Grave Seas

Palewell Press

Grave Seas

Hussam Eddin Baramo

Grave Seas

First edition 2021 from Palewell Press,

https://palewellpress.co.uk

Printed and bound in the UK

ISBN 978-1-911587-49-1

A CIP catalogue record for this title is available from the British Library.

Acknowledgements

Thank you to the late Charles Raybould, my friend at Hamlet Gardens. Without his wisdom, understanding and warm welcome, I would not have managed to find my way in London.

Thanks also to our great friends, Nermin Murad and Allan Garlick, who introduced us to more aspects to belonging and identity.

Many thanks for Camilla Reeve, Senior Editor of Palewell Press Ltd, for being a fantastic publisher and for showing the humane side of this industry that I worked for and loved to belong to all my life.

Thanks to Ismail Al-Rifai, Syrian poet and painter, for the beautiful painting on the front cover; to Khaldoun Al-Shamaa, my favorite literary critic; to Haifa Zangana, who for many decades has been a wonderful writer, poet and comrade; to Jabbar Yassin Hussin, amazing friend, poet and writer; and to Amir Darwish, who was the first to help with publishing this book.

Dedication

To Elfat, Julia-Leila and Sami

Words have no meaning without you

Diary kept by Winston in *"1984"*, George Orwell

"April 4th, 1984. Last night to the flicks. All war films. One very good one of a ship full of refugees being bombed somewhere in the Mediterranean. Audience much amused by shots of a great huge fat man trying to swim away with a helicopter after him…then you saw a lifeboat full of children with a helicopter hovering over it. there was a middle-aged woman might have been a jewess sitting up in the bow with a little boy about three years old in her arms. little boy screaming with fright and hiding his head between her breasts as if he was trying to burrow right into her and the woman putting her arms round him and comforting him although she was blue with fright herself, all the time covering him up as much as possible as if she thought her arms could keep the bullets off him. then the helicopter planted a 20 kilo bomb in among them terrific flash and the boat went all to matchwood…There was a lot of applause from the party seats but a woman down in the prole part of the house suddenly started kicking up a fuss and shouting they didn't oughter of showed it not in front of kids…until the police turned her out i dont suppose anything happened to her nobody cares what the proles say …"

Contents

Foreword – A Syrian riddle

There are some famous paintings depicting the meeting between "Oedipus and the Sphinx" as a fatal confrontation between a doomed human being and a mysterious creature who, through posing a riddle, holds the power to kill.

Oedipus had to answer the right words or he, and the whole people of Thebes, would die.

Thebes was the city of Cadmus, the Greek hero who was a Phoenician prince, being the son of Phoenix or Agenor (king of Phoenicia), the king of Tyre on the Syrian Mediterranean coastline. He was also the brother of Europa, who was abducted by Zeus and taken to the island of Crete where she gave birth to King Minos.

Taking in account this mixture of mythological and historical backgrounds, one can presume that Oedipus was a descendent of "Syrian migrants", albeit in different historical context than the one surrounding the Syrians who are fleeing their homeland to Greece right now.

For a Syrian, like myself, the whole road to my country has been, and always will be, filled with fatal riddles and dangerous words.

The most dangerous one, possibly, is the word **Syria** itself.

In the process of exchanging names and heroes, the Greeks were the first to use the word *Suria* interchangeably with another historical and geographical term, *Assuria*.

The Romans later made the right (or wrong?) distinction between the two terms. For them, Syria became *Bilad Ash-Sham,* a term that continued to be used by the Arabs (who took over the region from the Romans). *Bilad Ash-Sham* is the area between Asia Minor and Egypt. The two terms encapsulate, among many things, two major historical, geographical and religious aspects.

These two names/concepts have become a big wound inside the geographical and imaginative expansion that produced Cadmus, Europa and Oedipus as a united Mediterranean world and that helped to widen the way human civilizations exchange knowledge and produce mythologies to explain life, migrations and wars.

This region was given the name **Syria** again during the colonial period of nineteen century and this old/new name which is open to conflicting historical interpretations has been adopted gradually by many Syrians but mostly by nationalistic ideologues who were the first to try to solve the riddle of what Syria is and who the Syrians are.

So, it comes as no surprise that one of the nationalistic parties which was established in Mount Lebanon called itself the "National Social Syrian Party." This party tried to stage a military coup in Lebanon on 1st of July 1949 (following the example of another coup d'état in Syria on 31 March of the same year). The coup as crushed and its leader, Antoun Saada, a Greek Orthodox, was hanged (another coup will follow on the eve of 1961/1962 and will be crushed again). Fractions of the party are still exist until now.

Syria was under the Ottomans for centuries, hence all the early immigrants to the United States and Latin America were called Syrians or Turks and many of them, like their Phoenician ancestors who established Qarthage on the Tunisian coast, had managed to occupy powerful political and social positions in many Latin American countries.

Occupied by the French and British forces during World War I and by the early years after World War II, historical Syria ceased to exist.

A new riddle of two names was developed: Sykes and Picot (later we found out that it included a third one: Sergie Sazonov, the Russian Empire foreign minister before the 1917 revolution).

Those three diplomats signed a secret Asia Minor Agreement in 1916, which was revealed to the public a year later. The Bolsheviks published the agreement in the Russian newspapers 'Izvestia' and 'Pravda.' Three days later it was confirmed by the British 'Guardian.'

The colonial Sphinx, practically, defeated the Syrian Oedipus. Furthermore Syria, became a creature walks on four legs: the republics of Syria and Lebanon, the Hashemite kingdom and…the "want to be" Palestine state that was taken over by the Israeli forces in 1948 creating a new diversion of the great Syrian dilemma.

Those riddles inside riddles had sown the seeds of the apocalypse that we are witnessing now.

The creation of those states became the cause and the field of several wars, civil wars and continuous political, economic, sociologic and military turmoil, with gigantic tragic consequences in the region and the whole world.

***

In the newly created **Syrian Republic**, the French occupying forces divided Syria on ethnic and sectarian bases into five states, so we had a new five-legged creature. The Syrian Republic citizens managed to re-unite the country but they were wounded again by the separation of Lebanon and Jordan, and by what will be, in Modern Arab history, called the Palestinian Nakba.

This separation made most of the Syrians sympathise with the nationalistic propaganda and the military coups that kept popping up after the independence in 1946 until 1963 when a ruthless group of military officers took over under the slogans of socialism and the unity of the Arab countries, but, in fact, was a great opening to a very bloody tyranny under one man and his family that called the country "Syria of al-Asad."

Applying the Oedipus riddle to Syria, we might end the journey with some conclusions:

Humanity came from the same tree but we usually like to hide behind our small branches.

The Syrian riddle became a global one. The Syrians themselves became a metaphor for the human race. We are all crossing deadly borders and we all, to some degree, are in boats trying to reach somewhere. Many of us may die before completing the journey.

Civilization started with open borders, and the first immigrants brought with them the alphabet, trade and all sorts of knowledge; they were treated as heroes and were made kings. A whole continent was named after Europa, a princess from the Syrian coastal line, who could be identified, in today's terms, as an immigrant.

A new wave of "immigration" by force, which was called colonialism, came this time from Europe and sowed the seeds of new stage of civilization but also sowed seeds of political disputes, despair and destruction, if not by setting the infrastructure of military regimes and supporting tyrants.

The world is now facing a great riddle. Some of us are answering by becoming xenophobes and racists, some are building great walls to prevent others from coming, and some even are destroying the habitat of mother earth.

We either answer the riddle correctly or we, and the earth itself, are doomed.

English

My road to English started at Gatwick - 1994

The train halted in a flat at East London

I was born again at Hackney Empire

with-Turks, Kurds, Jews and Muslims all falling

                in love with English.

Another train dropped me at Westminster

where I had a military salutation by a Field Marshal

He told me that we are related:

He conquered the Middle East and defeated the Nazi

                Desert Fox.

Being a good soldier I froze in awe

Was that a jubilation or a humiliation?

Asking Shakespeare about the verb to be

a merchant from Damascus asked for a pound of my flesh.

I found another William Shakespeare.

killed in Arabia in 1915

helping the Saudis in their Game of Thrones

/continued

Alas, no one helped him with a horse to flee
and Robert De Niro mocked him in a film.

Standing next to Waxy Arab tyrants in Madam Tussauds
we were all smiling for the cameras.

My neighbor in Hammersmith had a nice name: Charles Darwin
The evolution of my English made us 'cool' friends.

In Agatha Christie's summer home
there was a mystery:
how did my aunt's Damascene chest of drawers come here?

A great historian told me to visit my ancestors in Cornwall:
Roman ancient soldiers from Palmyra.

I also found Jack the Ripper
drinking with a leftist gang praising a Syrian killer.

Waving farewell to a Damascene poet in Regent's Park Mosque
the Pakistani Imam greeted me by an Islamic speech in English.

My son became a fan of Arsenal
It was also the favorite team for Bin Laden!

In my English Odessa, I had to choose my political inclination:
"Coronation Street" or "Eastenders"?
The entangled drama kept running in my dreams
flashing with green Arabic subtitles.

I took a selfie in Trafalgar Square
but the photo did not show me.
It was the Last of the Moors' sighing:
We died in that place.

I took my family to "Les Misérables"
There we found our real selves.

We, finally, are English!

Trains

We tuck in our children's toys
hide them in the cracks of our falling country

We watch the birds of their souls
running back to Noah's boat.

We leave our grandfathers asleep under the oaks' hill
and say farewell to our shattered land.

We clean our homes before we leave
so the invaders enjoy our warm beds.

We carry wounds, slaps and insults and
from our bended shoulders
we free the god's wings
and fly far faraway

We track the ends of nights
and chase the farthest of borders.

We walk under water:
We are the Christs of drowned bodies.

Our mothers' prayers will save us from evil
And pull us from the placenta's yearnings.

We will slowly watch the vicious tyrants
Chasing the dreams of our genes.

We stray like dogs in Europe's fields
To flip the dice of our lives again.

We cross the Aegean Sea
A flood of a crazy Ulysses.

/continued

The trains take us to tents in Vienna

A river in Berlin

A jungle in France

And a grave in Hungary.

"Can we now go to sleep?", we ask our rescuers.

"We have to catch the next train."

The Soldier's Last Supper

I watch his eyes twinkling

like a blade slicing darkness

I kneel begging a crumb of pity

with downcast eyes... a defeated soul

just like my desecrated homeland

My ancestors' spirits are walking with me

chased out by invaders

their eyeball sockets glow with misery

I throw down the dice of my life

to lose, this time again, my hope

and to win, for the last time, my despair

Spinning like a spider

as it disintegrates, an eternal web

I will kneel on my tattered knees and

scatter upon my forehead the soil from this damned war.

/continued

I will gift my military pride
to the shoes of my enemy.

However, my enemy will not absolve
my enemy will not pardon
my own brother will not forgive
the brother who was fed at the same breast

the brother who played with me
on the swings of our destiny …

My brother will not be merciful with me
One of us has to be defeated
before he himself is defeated in turn
so that the president in a faraway palace may win.

One of us has to die

…so that the newsreader can glow as she reads the news of

impending victory

so that the hyenas at the royal banquet would wail and

the bold keeper at the cemetery would howl with terror.

I call him while he pulls his knife to slaughter me:

"My brother ... my brother" I scream

"My brother … my enemy.

Do you remember how we escaped the cane of our teacher?

and skipped away chasing the crows in winter?

Do you remember when we fell in love with the same girl?

and received a steady hail of slaps from her father.

Do you remember when we stole the cigarettes at the young

woman's funeral?

and cried as we considered the eternal beauty of her

deathly face?

/continued

Do you remember the passing cats shivering to death
                as we stroked their trembling soft fur?
listening to the birds' chirping before we bend
                their small heads?"

I am the mirror of my brother's hatred
I am the voice of his stunted speech
I am the shudder of his hand as he prepares to slaughter
and I… am the banner of his army
as it digs deeper into the back of my wounded motherland.

I am my beloved brother who is slaughtering me now
and leaving me headless … desolate
Together, we return to our mother
who
oblivious
awaits our laughter at dinner.

The boats are coming

I

Followed by the bees

to the road of honey.

Pulled by the scent of mad women

to the land of silk

we will only stop when we reach our deadly fate.

We are not going back.

We left our ageing fathers guarding their graveyards.

We cut our umbilical cords

from our motherland's womb

and dug down to the end of earth.

/continued

Heavy by our empty souls

we will cross the oceans' heart

we will sail the darkness sea

we will climb the vicious mountains

we will draw our childrens' gazes on the rocks

break the beast of mean waters

and cross.

Europe has died

Herodotus became a history.

Paul marked the Road from Damascus

to the apocalypse

and gave us our beastly promised land.

II

We lived in strange people's houses
We borrowed their happy stories
We slept in their wives' beds
We also stole their lovers
We pretended to be their children's parents
and we wore their clothes.

But our nightmares followed us
Our mocking grandfathers chased our shadows
We then sat hopeless at the gloomy shores
waiting for our boats
to take us back again.

Lost ship

You do not reach wisdom, in the last years of your life,
                    by being wise
Your wisdom is nothing but organizing the affairs
                of a great mischief.
You should, instead, repeat your starting sins:
to gurgle with joy of the defiled milk
to follow the smells of malicious pleasures
to chase the crazy cats of instincts
to moan the dark alley hooker who forsook you
to write a love poem but the girl runs away from you
                    to the end of earth
to be crushed by a cruel song that throws you like hay
to offer yourself to answer the riddle of life,
but find yourself outside it
to follow an idiot party
that want to change the world
to find that the world did change but the party has not
to run in order to complete your poem
but find out that you destroyed your life.

Climb aboard you miserable poet

Your fractured wisdom ship to the great ocean of no wisdom.

Help the wolf

Do not praise the kindness of the butterfly
She might be a camouflaged beast.

Do not criticize the cruelness of the hyena
He may be longing to become a lamb.

Do not follow the bees' trail
if you are not a fan of bitterness.

Do not water the fish flower
She will run away from you to the sea.

Do not enter the spider's web
if you know how to get out.

Do not follow Noah's dove
You might find your promised land.

Do not accuse the snake

You are the one who stole the apple.

Do not blame the passing dog

It was your brother who cut your flesh.

Give the crocodile's tears a chance

He might be overseeing your coming funeral.

Give the devil a chance

God might revert the story.

Support the wolf in his trial

You were the one who killed Joseph.

Do not break the tree

Its branches will feed from your bones.

Do not be afraid of the hanging eagle

It does not know that you will die today.

Damascene sword

I

Farther and farther

the North trains are taking us

from the bedroom into St Fillans' village

from the navel of imaginary home

to the towns where two strangers have never been.

Flying through the sea vagueness

British Airways

will take our single soul

into two directions.

We come back from the night

trembling in the mountain hotel's car

reaching out for the thread of passion.

intoxicated by the perfume of Scottish pine

Strangers will become lovers.

Our clothes will moan in the cottage

The trees womb will embrace us

Our laughter will shake the candles

The squirrels tread on dawn

The stairs coil

The rain falls

The dust scatters

We fall into water

into the core of meaning

uncovering what our soul has left behind

in the grave depth of Loch Earn.

II

We dance

to the music of Theodorakis

We melt into each other with the rhythm of Salsa

We are on the knife-edge of happiness

I will not make love to the Brazilian dancer

You will not get jealous and crazy.

Our howling is making waves in the mountain

A herd of tigers conquering a forest

Our wild fire flaming the place.

Seduce me with your accent

with the desire for a child

with the hope for a future

We will ignore the past though

it will always point at us with a Damascene sword.

III

Dear Christiana, guardian of the park
the artist of self-locked spirits.
Leipzig rose bending with the green lines

Picture the colours of that:
A drop of rain comes from Damascus by God's Express Mail
clashing with a melancholic Russian song
translated by a communist abstract painter from East Germany
tells us stories of sailors in love with seafaring.

God bless you my father the traveler.
What a tumultuous seed you sowed in me
like a commandment
that made me leave the egg of Islam in the cold
embarking on a pilgrimage to heavenly Christiana's Lakes.

IV

Here we are on a defeated war

disarmed on Homer's land

our banner torn to shreds, amulets and riddles

our enigma is that we are here

that our children are our forthcoming murderers.

Pray for the hopeless dead

Pray for the great malicious deeds

Let this watery death come upon us

Would our ancestors bless us?

Would peace be upon us?

We have won!

As we are dragging our light slight bodies

on an endless journey towards the final loss.

Missed call

"I don't love you," said the woman on the phone.

"Crazily," she added.

"The line is cut, why you are listening?"

"Check my heart's signal with your pulse,"

"When I am dead, don't make me laugh,"

"Touch me when the birds flee!"

"Touch me please!"

"Why I am blue and my eyes are black?"

"When you hear me cry bring some air,"

"I am afraid the cry won't be enough,"

"I am dead now. Can you clearly hear my voice?"

Sleeping beauties

I met her in a course to learn hypnotism.

We decided to practice with each other.

In my turn, I ordered her to be my lover.

In her turn, she ordered me to be her lover.

We slept on love orders and no one woke us up.

*

Our children are now asleep.

The dead people's game

The bombardment stopped

The children went out.

A wounded pigeon landed limping

One of them suggested:

"Let's play the fighters' game."

Holding the pigeon, he started whistling.

Another one had a better idea

"Let's play the game of dead people."

They spread their bodies on the ground and laughed.

When the fighters came back

heading to the children's village

throwing an exploding barrel

The pigeon fled and flew.

The children's thoughts hovered above them:

"Are we children playing the dead people game

or this is our souls flying in the air?"

The happy cemetery

From my home inside a cemetery
I watch the dead:

A wife trying, in vain, to move her husband
He, again, is on top of her.

A child is trying to reach out to her plastic doll
As she fails, her pupils glow with shreds of green glass
her wheat legs are crushed with an invisible sickle.

A young boy tries to flirt with the new girl in the block
Lovely spiders curry his sweet words
while her body shivers with holy joy.

A man tries, every night, to get his kitchen knife
to protect his daughter from vicious hunters.
He fails and, again, sees them raping her.

The soldiers who were buried in haste

try daily

to hide their arms and flee to their wives.

All the dead, young and old

try, at daybreak, to get out of their graves to breath air.

Some want only to smoke a cigarette before returning

happily to the humid earth.

Some have bigger dreams.

Something, nevertheless, keeps preventing them.

Every day I try to say good night to my dead friends

and like them, I can't.

Some people are meeting to decide what to do with

the cemetery

Witnesses and sightseers are, cheerfully, watching.

Predicting the past

I am the helmet of sorrows

I predict the past

I wake the dead from deep nightmares.

I recall the ambassadors of astrology

to count the flour of skulls

I hit the stars with an eloquent mandala

of dead lovers' smoke

I reduce what left from what is rising.

I pull my spells from the spirits' beads

I save the salamander, the lizard and snake

from their doomed burrows

press my talismans on the falling planets.

I have work to do

before the language dies

and the great game of fates collapses.

1

Mohammad, my father, slept while in the bus
A passenger tried to bring him back from his light dream
Being my father only, not Jesus, he did not come back
        after three days.
There was an extra fault in the passenger's abilities to resurrect
        the dead so, they could not wake him up.
He won his nice sleep in the white 14 of February
        so I loved him
once for he is my father, and another for leaving me
        on Valentine's Day.
In that vehicle, leaving to the end, he spoke to me
He asked me to do what I always do: keep on travelling.

2

I remember, my dad, your first absence.

I remember, maybe, your warm robe made from small lambs

sleeping in my grandfather's lap

I wish to remember our journeys.

Taking me to the genie's ally.

Tucked with imaginary bleating lambs

we descend into the small cross where the horror of

evil creatures

was impersonated by the government's Mokhabarat.

Your shadow extends, my absentee dad, and mixes with

blue painted windows to camouflage our home

from Israeli fighters in 1967.

Your shadow became you, suddenly, and we became inhabitants

of open skies with train tracks, wheat fields, frogs

and anchovies.

I remember, dad, your final absence.

3

My soul is flying over a land and small heavens

A happy cinema director pulls my embryo's cord

trying to get over my fish heritage

I hold the thread of memory

a smell of my mother's milk

flies with the full ballooned sky

I hear the shrieking of my aunties dreaming of a small tribe

hovering over all that

my soul tries to remember where were you, my dad:

in the house bordering the cemetery

in al-Mojtahed hospital near Michael Aflaq's home?

in my grandfather who came from Jordan

or my grandfather who came from Aleppo?

Death is fading the memory

so, do not trouble yourself to remember

I shall remember for all of us

/continued

Trying to pull your sad head from a laughing death
the peculiar accident comes back again:
The son who became a father
who saw himself in his father's pictures
who left a photo for his son so he might see you
and write you this poem.

Another Year's Eve

Pouring my cold coffee into a broken handled cup

In another year's eve

Of: a square table carrying cards that no one has sent

Of: I do not want to call anybody

Of: hesitating to reply

Of: fear of losing (or winning) betrayal

Of: a look that cannot describe this laughing rain

Hitting the windows of "Hamlet Gardens"

Another year of leaving the tree's leaves on my forsaken books

Let's call it "the tree of no one sending presents"

Let's call Christmas another name

Like:

The day an orphan boy was told that God is his dad

Or

The holy day of the beautiful past years and the miserable future

ones

Or

The day of the woman who will regret visiting me tonight?

The hedgehog

We didn't expect this Christmas to arrive

but Jesus was born and we are still alive

fighting our way through swarms of shoppers,

Sainsbury's believers and Costco's worshippers,

Humanity struggling to get its daily booze

and each one's share of sex and blues.

All got drunk on 2021's eve

so I consumed my year's end grief.

Instead of asking for a yearly flu jab

did I enquire the nurse about my dose of 'blowjob'?

The pandemic made us scared

so we gathered to make the knowledge shared:

a conservative English faithful atheist,

a revolutionary Muslim breaching the laziest,

a Swedish Syrian from a gnostic sect,

whose ancestors came from China while they slept,

a friend from Jordan, three sisters from Al-Jazeera

and three youths who swear by Shakira.

We could not follow to the same TV songs,

elders' classics clashed with rapping young

so we watched Netflix, each in our own room

as the Christmas tree stayed in our living room.

The adults were descending so the money drop from sky

while young ones only wanted to flow too high.

To make a lovely ending to the headless day

without too much bending in an endless play

all insisted on giving me a hug

not one of them noticing

the thorns that are popping

out of me: the prickly hedgehog.

The garden Buddha

Running inside the roots,

the earth hears my complaint:

"I am the tree salt",

I say.

"the waste of nature,

the navel of the well."

I surrender my fragility to the ground

disappear in the radish,

in the cucumber,

in the leaves of the zucchini,

the dew of its yellow petals.

My trunk hides a cold cat

My fringe play with the snails

My body to be a child's chair

My red vine's spirit to the thirsty.

A clouded rock embraced me

I slept in my long grass

woke up in my weak tree

I saw lights when my coal glowed

I decided to get down:

I took off my human cloth

Dressed the gown of earth

and dissolved to a soil

My mother watered me

My leaves shot up

An embryo in the womb of the garden started to grow

I saw the dawn trembling like a virgin

I witnessed a baleful light

The night bowed its head

for the light

/continued

I saw myself

under the rain

Years went on

while I was asleep

in the festival of earth

Watching the chlorophyll

running into my veins

I see the grains of life flourishing

while existence embrace the nothingness.

Dead Poets Society

I am going to pass this life today.

Farewell, my friends in the "Dead Poets Society."

all six hundred thousand and fifty of you,

who are planning to vanish with me.

What a joyful journey we had!

We sat under Siddhartha's tree and fouled under it

We followed the Lamb of God and were intoxicated

                by his death.

We attacked kings and played fools.

Now, it is time to change the course.

Armed with our angry ancestors

we rise in the darkest of illusions

from our hidings

in the hens' coops

to conquer the vast lands of humans.

/continued

Legions of knights on wooden horses

Armies of rhythmic tanks.

Our songs' of foot soldiers fed with sorrows

Our sonatas' armors swayed with bitterness.

We blessed women with immaculate conceptions

We divided paradise among refugees

We spiced our failing lives

with metaphors and oratory.

Dante is watching us from his hell

The camels eat Al-Mutannabi's sword

The goats climb Rambo's rifles

while, like hordes of locusts,

we race time

to solve the secret of existence.

We are now heading to the sea

to surrender our flags

sink our ships

and, before taking our wretched souls to the dark abyss,

we will take a last gaze of hopelessness.

Hussam Eddin Baramo – Biography

Journalist and writer, Hussam Eddin Baramo (Email: Syrian.writerz@gmail.com) was born in 1961 in Al-Meedan, the southern suburb of Damascus. A formative childhood experience was visiting 'Dar Al-Oloum', his father's press house, where he was intrigued by the smell of industrial ink and paper, the noise of printing machines spitting hot books. Hoping for a better life and a liberal political system, the family moved to Lebanon in 1969. This transition was the first in a series of cultural, political and geographical changes that would influence his writings. After the 1975 outbreak of the Lebanese Civil War, his family decided he should return to his grandfather's house in Damascus in order to complete his studies.

On his journey home, he witnessed lines of Syrian tanks approaching Lebanon, and this incident set the tone for the years ahead in Syria. Hussam entered college to study politics and economics and, during a visit to Beirut, became a member of a small Marxist party. With another leftist clandestine group, he continued his involvement in this line of dangerous politics in Syria. By co-founding a publishing company, Al-Wa'I, in Damascus in 1986, he went back to his father's roots, publishing books by renowned writers such as Ghaleb Halasa, Mamdouh

Edwan, and Ahmad Fouad Nijm. Having endured the repression that crushed Syria and his party, and imprisoned many of his friends, in 1989 he moved to Cyprus to work as an editorial secretary for a political women-oriented magazine called Shehrezad in Limassol. In 1994 he moved to the UK where he has lived since then, working for a London-based Arabic newspaper.

When the Syrian uprising against the Syrian regime began in 2011, he was part of the creation of the Syrian Writers Association, and served as vice-president and editor-in-chief of Awraq, its cultural publication (2012-2019). He is a columnist, political analyst and has been a speaker at universities, conferences, TV programmes and seminars as well as contributing to debates.

Hussam's previous publications include a poetry book, *Poisoned Kohl*, 2012, and short stories. He translated *Introduction to Slavoj Zizek* and *Post Orientalism*, by Hamid Dabashi, 2013. At present, he works as Managing Editor of Al-Quds Al-Arabi newspaper.

Palewell Press

Palewell Press is an independent publisher handling poetry, fiction and non-fiction with a focus on books that foster Justice, Equality and Sustainability. The Editor can be reached on enquiries@palewellpress.co.uk